AND OTHER POEMS BY J. ANDREW THOMAS

Also by J. Andrew Thomas

Suburban Purgatory Hell
Mauled by Death in the Hot Rain
Staring into the Void of Destruction
College is for Losers (Novel)
The Garden Gnomes are Watching
Sometimes You Get Lucky and the Problem Fixes Itself
Poems for Another Day
Cattle Prod (Novel)
All My Friends are on Television
Swallow God Swallow Nothing
With Pugs
The Bastards Will Always Win
Non-Union (Novel)
Ocean Currents (Play)
She Catches Her Breath in a Sob (Play)
The Greats are not so Great
A Place To Go When Things Went Wrong (Play)
Dead End Poems
Empire of Nothing (Novel)
Back to the Bars
Let Me Hold Your Heart Like a Flower (Play)
Dumb But Not Quite Damned
*The Loud Thunderous Roar of Girls Searching For Invisible Love
(Play)*
It's Not Going to Get Better Only More Comfortable
Pitchfork (Novel)
Spring in Shamrock (Novel)
To Darkness Through a Wreath of Sudden Pain (Novel)
Wallowing in Obscurity
For a Second (Screenplay)

Nothing Doing Here There Anywhere
Bad Design
Her Candle so expire (Novel)
The Fat of the Day (Play)
Looking Down From Below
One Win Choice (Screenplay)
Spider in a Forest Fire
People Were Smaller Back Then (Play)
Super Busy Doing Absolutely Nothing
Three Porches (Play)
Sheep Drive
A Short Farewell (Play)
Hank and Emma and Sometimes Leo
We Should Not Expect Them to Be What We Want Them to Be
The Protected Wild (Novel)
To the Crowd (Short Stories)
See the World Burn
The Tail End of (play)
Time Again Later
Some Peace (play)
from a flowerless land
Says You (play)

Punching into Nowhere

nothing changes

"he fucking sucks,"
I said. "no way he makes it through the year."

"total. he's a high school coach, all these
Belichick guys never pan out. they are all
frauds," Ralph said.

and there we were again
at 40
trashing the guy from our high school who
went on to coach in the NFL

"can't believe they are paying him 5 mil."

"it's ridiculous. I don't even know why he
took the job."

"who wouldn't for that kind of money? even if he only
coaches 2 years it's worth it!"

"I guess. could have waited a little while longer
he doesn't have enough experience."

"and then what? maybe he wouldn't get another
offer. he had to take it."

"he's still an idiot."

"yes."

and it felt good. really good. we were the idiots

but it made us forget about our stupid
ordinary lives for a bit

us poor fuckers
who will never amount to anything
saying how this guy who beat the odds
who made it out of our stupid town
to make millions in the NFL to
be famous

he's he moron.

hahahahahahaha. god are we dumb. but
that's high school

well never get out of that mentality. we
can't. it's in us forever.

we see it but we don't want to believe

when you see it was 67 degrees
in Alaska
on December 25th
beating out the previous high of 45 degrees
on the same day in 1984
it's hard to think about the long term future
or care about anything other than
the upcoming weekend and how much
fun we can have
because
we all know were beyond fucked
and
it's only a matter of time
until shit gets bad and a good number
of the human race living in America
is contemplating mass suicide
over living in a world
where we can't have everything
all the time.

nothing here

up in this brain
it's empty

                                       finally. it feels so good
I am like them
they finally got me
just
exist
don't think
it doesn't matter. the world is done…why
keep typing
like this?

it's useless. become them. they are happy. so dumb
and happy
I will be there soon. just stop typing. NOW. STOP
YOU MOTHER FUCKER!

safe and sound

reading about people dying
horrifically

by murder and by accident
or
by sickness

just
normal people
living life
and then

boom!

FUCKING DEAD…it really convinces you
that
the end is coming soon
and there's nothing you can do about it
which
really makes you think carefully about
every action you take in life…and it's no
wonder I don't go out much
anymore.

how many sitting at the typer
or
watching old movies on VHS tapes
or
in the basement playing pool and
Nintendo

have suddenly died?

I don't hear about any
and
that's the way
I'm going to keep it.

it's what they do

"real Christmas tree, right?" I said.

"yeah, it was huge, like 12 feet high!" she said.

"oh yeah, I knew it! that's rich people shit
right there."

"why?"

"they don't do cheap fake trees. it's always a beautiful
giant real tree that shows how high their ceilings are. it's what
they do. shows their wealth."

"oh."

John < Paul

we all love Joh Lennon
when we are young
he's the rebel
he's the dickhead
he's the genius
and then
we get a little older, wiser, calmer
and
then we realize
the gentle Paul
was the real genius
he was responsible for more
of the music
than
John
and for once in the history of man
the good guy
got to live longer
and the shithead
went to the grave.

funny thing

we thought back in the 70's and 80's that
in the 90's
and 2000's we would be in flying cars
and holograms would be a major thing
and
robots would be all over the place
and
maybe even time travel!

and
now
it's just people
dressed in sweat pants and
hoodies in sandals
looking like homeless people
in every mode of life
while
staring at our phones all day
and
we have to check ourselves out at the store
because
people don't want to work

that's the future
and
2050
will be pretty much the same
only
worse…

all this chaos

on display
all it takes
is a few clicks and we can see the most
horrific things you will ever see
real murder and rape and burnings and
car crashes and people losing their minds
on a daily basis

and I'm just sitting here
at the job
nice and warm

not really moved
one way or another

all I want is a long and uneventful life.

just boring as hell. it's too much of a risk
to get involved in anything anymore.

people are unraveling at an unbelievable
pace.

and
there is no cure all. it's a god damn cycle
were in. we turn on the stupid internet
box and see it all and it either infuriates us
or makes us jealous or horrified and scared
and we can't help but go a little mad
each day that passes.

I'll be here though. looking like I'm in a fish tank
out into the world. nothing can hurt me in here
in this calm and stable life. I don't want to go
out and do anything. I have my house and my job and the
wife and the child and
fishing and the grocery store and TV and video games
and writing and reading good books and my fish tank
and painting terrible pictures and mowing the lawn and the
old Chevy's and the beer, oh the beer, how could I forget the
beer. it's
a peaceful existence. in this small aquarium. it's warm. it's
mine. nobody can take it away, except, well…

you know.

they are here to stay

you thought you were done with those childish video games
because you temporarily moved on to more mature
adult responsibilities and they took hold of your life and there
was no damn time to sit around and reminisce about the
stupid past but now you have some free time and it's winter
and cold as fuck and you have your office back and it's
morning and everyone is sleeping and the coffee is hot and
you are a lazy piece of shit who should be lifting weights in
the basement but it's Friday, fuck it, I'm relaxing, watching it
snow,
scrolling through the list of 8 bit wonders that
you were obessed with at age 10 and
it's just like you are back there, with no care about anything
else going on in the world and you know this won't last
forever, it will get old soon or something else will come
along and take you away, some stupid bullshit that
is meaningless as playing these games
but
you will keep them in the back of your mind
because
it's the only way to time travel
out of this terrible
world we are living in.

albino gorillas

I'm amazed by these type
of guys
they walk around with gusto and fervor and
authority
at work
and
they run into the bathroom
and
drop their pants and are shitting before they sit down

how do they do it?

they have no time
they
just blow out their asses and
they are back to work in 30 seconds

meanwhile
I'm back at home

hoping I can get off the bowl
in less than 10 minutes…

punching into nowhere

I trudged in
on Sunday
like I always did
but it was harder
now that the football season
had started.

I punched into nowhere
and was immediately
met with the smell of
microwave popcorn
floating through the air.

I walked into the breakroom
and saw it was filled
to the brim
with the same bunch of
brawlers
talking loudly,
watching football and
anxiously running out the clock.

it was the two minute warning,
the end was near
and they had enough
of work
and life.

I found a spot in the corner
and read

my book,
sipping on cold
purified water
waiting for them
to clear out
so I could think.

a table over
I heard a bald, fat man
yelling at another
fat man
wearing a football jersey.

"I am not taking your bullshit anymore!" baldy yelled.

"if you try anything, I am going to put
in a grievance!" jersey yelled back.

they looked like
two big rams
sizing each other up
ready to strike.

the yelling used to
bother me
it stung my ears
like an
angry wasp

as the days became
years
the behavior
became normal

it didn't even phase me
anymore

I understood why
they acted like
children.

years and years
at this place
have torn them down
made them bitter as
a scorned lover.

it was a battle here
every day,
every god damn day.
company vs union,
they never stopped.

I sat on the bench
watching it all
unfold
not caring which
team
won or
lost.

for the love

whenever we start doing something
                              cool
like sports or
writing
or
music
or
art
or
film making

we picture ourselves as a genius famous
person
who was once the best in the world
at the craft

like Jordan or
Hemingway
or
Bonham
or
Picasso
or
Kubrick

and the whole time we are doing it
we think once we put in enough time
we will rise to the same heights as those
giants
and it's great that we think this
even though it's completely insane

because
most likely we are just average
average
average
people
like everyone else
just passionate
and that's ok
but
it keeps us going
and then
one day
after years or weeks or months

we look at ourselves and what were doing and
think

is it worth it?

is this worth our time?

nothing is happening…so should we continue?

you won't ever make it at this
you will have to work a job the rest of your life…

you will never be famous…nobody will ever know you…

and here we are
still typing poems that nobody will ever read…just

FOR THE LOVE OF THE GAME…

Mr. Hanky the Christmas Poo

watching the South Park Christmas Special
like the old days
when I was with the ex-wife
(it was a yearly tradition)
I can't get through it, it's too hard, I can't do it,
I can't time travel, all I do is think of her and how
young we were and carefree and how good things
were and how different we thought things would
end up
so I shut it off and feel a little sad for a while
and then
I see the baby smile
and it all goes away…things…they kind of worked out…

didn't they?

for whatever reason that is

we think when we retire, we are going to get to do
all the cool shit we wanted to do our whole lives and
never had the time
but
the reality is we won't be doing anything, we will be tired
and achy and possibly sick or most likely we will be dead
but
if we do make it
we won't be doing shit, we will be eating and napping and
watching TV and hoping we don't get cancer like
all our friends
that's the reality, nobody is doing anything, they are all
hanging on by a thread

just happy they are still
alive.

leave us alone

they try and tell us gambling is the devil, it will make you go
broke and you will lose your soul but then I think about the
famous Norm MacDonald who went broke many times
because he was addicted to gambling and yet he died a few
months ago and seemed very comfortable and battled cancer
for 9 years and yet he wasn't living on the street
so
maybe
it can happen
you can live a whole life and gamble the whole time and win
and lose and never make a dime but still be really entertain
and stressed and feel like you are alive
and then
you die
with 7 dollars to your name and it doesn't matter
so
get off our back
us old gamblers
we know what were doing
we might lose 250 in a weekend but
the next one
well make it all back
plus
30
so
fuck off!

no more pressure

Billy Joel
has stated
in an interview
he's done writing new songs
and that made me very happy
because old rock stars who have a million hits
shouldn't try and make new music in their late
60's
it's not going to ever be good again
and I think I might be getting to that place
as well
even though I never wrote anything good
I did type with some insane fervor
when I first started
and
now
it's very different
it's more of a struggle and isn't as fun
so
I'll give it a little while longer
and see
if things change. if not…I'll go the way of Billy. it's just
easier…

"let's go out to breakfast"

might be the five worst words
to hear
on a dreary Sunday morning
feeling shitty and bloated
head pounding
joints aching

all you want to do is get a cup of coffee
and
sit on the couch and not have to do anything
but
she's smiling and it's been a damn long
time since we've
been out early in the morning
fuck
you gotta do it, there's no way out
of this one
so
you fill your cup and mosey upstairs and
sit on the bowl for a while
and feel a little better
get dressed
put on deodorant
a hat
and
a hoodie
and then go downstairs and say

"ready to go?"

and then she looks so happy

because she assumed I wouldn't
want to go
and I still don't
but that doesn't matter
she's happy
so
I'm happy.

forgotten heroes

every year
those sorry garbage men
put a card in the trash can lid
around Christmastime
hoping to get a tip
and
every year, I take that card inside and put it on the
counter and tell
myself
I'm going to pick up some cash and put a crisp
10 dollar bill
in there
and then
all year they will remember I thought of them
even though
it's really nothing
but
it's *something…*

and then
a week after the New Year
I open the island drawer and
see the forgotten card in there
waiting for that bill
and
now it's too damn late
and again
I feel like a food

those trashmen
if anyone deserves some extra

cash around the dreadful holidays
it's them

and like most everyone else
like the asshole I am
I forgot.

we take it for granted
that
when we put out a mound of waste
it gets magically taken away
by these men
who endure all the fucking elements
more so than
mailmen
who
I *never* forget to tip
each year
and they don't have to go
home
smelling like shit everyday
which
makes no fucking sense
other than we don't really think of those
guys who make a living hauling
trash
as real people…but then
recently you were home
during the week
and you see them pull up to the curb in their
truck
a big arm comes out and grabs the bin
and dumps it in the back

and then it's compacted
all without them leaving their warm
truck
as the guy in the passenger seat is playing
on his phone…you don't feel so bad
because
it's not like the old days where some guy was hanging
off the back
trying not to get killed by oncoming traffic
getting off at each house
hoisting the cans in
garbage juice going everywhere
cars beeping as they hurry to work…it's
gotten a little better for them
hasn't it?

he used to be the butt of everyone's jokes

the fool
the bumbling idiot
the man nobody wanted to associate with
the big joke

but then
his dad died

was murdered
in cold blood

an innocent

                                  unlucky old man

and now
now
we all feel sorry for him

he's a real person now. we don't think about him
like we did last week

it's impossible. we put ourselves in his
shoes
and
we can't talk behind his back anymore

we see the error in our ways…but we have
shifted focus on others now…it's automatic
we can't help it…we need someone to step on
because that's how life works…there has to be someone
below us

who make ourselves feel
better
about our stupid
pointless lives
sitting here
at this place
against our will
only
to
survive.

they were all over

those stupid arrowheads
we found
walking the creek
we thought nothing of them
oh cool, an Indian made this to kill some animal
and
we took it home and put it on a shelf
and
now I think about it
it's amazing!
finding that shit
something maybe hundreds of years old
crafted by some primitive simple man
and
now it's on my shelf…

we don't know back then

the biggest fear of youth when getting in relationships
is it becoming boring and stale, it's worse than death to
us
and then
you get old or older and then you figure out that every
relationship will get moldy will come to a standstill
no matter what

and you don't give a fuck about anything and it feels so
GREAT!
but
then
you think about how life really mattered back then. and then
you get sad…because shit did matter at one point in your
life…

let it go

we think well retire and have all this energy and time
to do all the things we wanted to do our whole lives and
it's going to be amazing
and then I see these workless bastards and they don't
want to do anything, all they want to do is
                                    nap and eat
and I don't blame them
life is fucking hard
you are tired
give up
give it up
it's not worth it

poor is cool

reading his drunken poetry
about being poor as hell
living with horrible women
getting into fights
people being murdered all around him
dealing with terrible depression and anxiety
and anger…it's delightfully enjoyable
sitting in my nice house in front of a gas
lit fire
below my 65 inch HD TV…and then
you turn on your phone and read a story
about a man who was living in a cheap
rented room at a shit Quality Inn
20 minutes away…the drunken bastard
beat his 3 kids and wife and nearly
killed them…that's the reality of 99.9% of
these drug addicts and alcoholics…this
one guy who managed to depict his lifestyle
living on skid row
into a literary career…well that's a one in a billion
lucky bastard and shouldn't be taken
seriously
because there are some really dangerous fuckers
running around out there
and
I'm happy never to have lived that life…it's not
the 1960's anymore…you can't be poor and get by on the
streets without being some fucking mental
patient…life is insanely expensive nowadays and if you
if you don't kill yourself every fucking day working
you will be dead in a year…

it looked like an interesting article

about some German chemical company
and how their manufacturing plants in the
United States, the ones that made dishwashing
liquid

                              a big brand that everyone
knows…

…and how they were poisoning the environment
the water and the air
and how it was affecting the people
who lived nearby…

I scrolled for a few seconds
trying to get the gist
very quickly
and then
when I saw that the article was very long
I clicked out.

those things used to have me glued to the
words
but now, now, now, I simply don't care
anymore. there's nothing I can do about it
and even if there was, I wouldn't do anything
because it doesn't directly affect my life. something
might be out there, something in the future, some kind
of horrible shit that is coming for me or my family
and then I'm going to have to deal with that, like these
bastard German fucks. but for me to spend my precious
hours
getting all worked up about the rich assholes who run

the world and don't give a damn about anybody…it's just
a waste of time and the anxiety and sadness it causes
isn't worth it anymore.

I only have so many hours on this earth and I feel like
I could die at any moment, I can't
keep focusing on the bad, even though, it's so
damn easy and gratifying in a way.

and yet
looking around
trying to find some good
outside of my house

seems to be getting harder and harder
as each day
goes by…

plants are people

and don't forget it

you put those fuckers together
they are happy
you play them music
they are happy
you talk to them
they are happy
you give them water
they are happy

so
prove me wrong!

these guys

who don't have regular jobs
who
quit drinking
all say they can't get fucked up on the
weekends like
normal people
hahahahahahahahaha
they
don't get it! they have too much free time!
we all have to get up at 5am and go to work
so we
keep it in check!
they can't
they can't
they never will
so
they need to stop entirely
which is hilarious
because
us
poor fucks
who show up
a little hungover and
do a lot of complicated shit
sometimes
at work
we
we
have it down. and that's a damn skill.

back in high school again

as I stand behind her in line
I already know how it's going to go
she will walk by
and not even see me. we have lived in the same
neighborhood for 2 plus years and
she jogs or walks with her kids by
my house
a few times a week and she has to know
what I look like, that I'm a person
who lives right down the street from her
but
maybe not? maybe I'm that invisible. this is
the girl who went to my high school, who
walked around the halls looking like hot
shit
who didn't knew I existed back then
and
now she turns to walk past me
and
a glance is given for a second and then she
looks away
like it's the first time she has ever seen me
and
I'm back in high school again but this time
I am so devoid of any want of human
interaction
I just smirk and say to myself it's always
going to be this way, nobody ever breaks out
of high school
it's impossible!
I should care but I do!

we all do!
anybody who says any different is fucking
lying!

I get it

we've all had enough of this shit
this
present time
it's awful
it's shit
so
let's just go back to another time
when
we were younger
it wasn't better
it
was just
we were younger and life was fun
so
let's go back
it's warm and comfortable and
it makes us feel good
so
fuck it
you have the present
I'll be
living in the past
where
it's fun as shit. fuck you all!

**if we ran into each other at the store
I don't know what I would say**

I'll be going along
with life
my new life
my good life
my easy life
my amazing life
not thinking about
the bad shit that I went through
years ago
and then
I drive by
the doctors office where SHE works
(5 min down the street)
and
I see her name
on there
with my last name (she kept it)
and
there I am
back there
in that place
but
instead of thinking of all that horrible
shit we went through
I just
focus on all the good stuff
the
fun we had
that first year
while she was still in art school

all that fucking we did
and
drinking and smoking cigarettes
and
talking about the future
and
how good it was going to be
together

I keep thinking she will eventually
get a new job
and
one day I'll drive by and her name will be gone
but
it's been 5 fucking years!

she might
be there forever
but
I haven't seen her anywhere around town
so
I'm happy about that.

don't be fooled

by the constant complaining of
bartenders
who say they hate their job and dealing with
drunks
all night long is such an unforgiving and
thankless job.

it's all bullshit. they love it. they love every minute of
it. they can't work a regular job so this is what they
do and as we all know, we can't help but complain
about any job we're chained to
but
most of us
don't post pictures
looking all cool at our jobs
wearing sunglasses, pouring drinks with kooky
hair
dancing around
with the hashtag *#lifeofabartender*
telling everyone how many cool and interesting
people we meet on a nightly basis…no
no
no
most of us show up and work early in the morning
just happy to be awake enough to do our shitty job
and hear endless
awful chatter from our co-workers who live
worse lives than ourselves
and then
it's lunchtime! a shining happy moment in then
comes the awful

afternoon hangover
very sleepy
just trying to trudge through until 2pm when we can
have a cup of coffee to help get us through until
5pm
where we sit in traffic for a half hour
hungry as hell
wishing it was Friday so we could have a drink
and then
you get home and say FUCK IT
I'm going to have a glass of wine with dinner and
then
2 bottles later you are
going to be an hour too late
and then
you hear that alarm and realize…it's only
Wednesday.

no
we all can't have the *#lifeofabartender*.

that little smile

is what is going through my brain

the world is an awful awful afwul
place
where we are trapped
and
it's never getting any better
the end is coming soon
and
there's nothing we can do about it!

is what is going through my brain
on a daily basis

and then
that little guy

he gives me that smile
from across the room
as he cruises from
the couch to the end table
with a toy in his hand
and everything else
fades
nothing else exists in life
and
I'm healed.

everything is going to be ok. it's like
a magic antidote
to this

terrible poison
we call LIFE!

for so long I avoided
a baby and
now I realize
it's been that missing puzzle piece
the whole time!

before writing

life was so easy and simple and
mindless

just go to work and go home and
don't go broke and drink
on the weekends and
                 fuck when you can
and
watch lots of TV and movies and
                 read when you can

and
go out to eat and go to the city or go bowling and
                 go on vacation when you can

and
be happy that you aren't sick and you aren't bored
                 and visit family when you can

and
just be.

that was it.

just be

and now
there's this nagging feeling
I get
whenever I am enjoying myself
doing any one of those things above

that I enjoy
oh so very much
that
I shouldn't be doing that thing. I should be writing. I should
be crafting a new story or play or writing terrible poems
and it's
not good for me. it's not. so
it may be time to let it go for a while. see what happens.

then
in a few months
go back
and
maybe I will enjoy it again.

that's what I've found works for most things
even
people
and
I think many people would agree.

control

now
he's here
this
beautiful baby
I've finally figured it out
to
get to that place
in between
totally wasted
and
barely drunk
it's a good place
it's a safe place
it's a warm place
it's better than ok
but
not as good as the place
I got
in college
where
all the world went away
while smoking 8 million cigs
but
that can't last forever
just
a little fun
is
better than
none at all.

crazed poet

John Hinckley, the crazy
asshole who shot Reagan
who
was obessed with Jodi Foster
who
turned out to be a lesbian

well
he was a poet
and
after he went to jail
the band
DEVO
stole a line
from one of his
poems
and
now
40 years later
he wants money
so
that just goes to show
if you
are a poet
you
need to
do some crazy shit
to actually
get recognized
if not
if you are some loser

in the suburbs
who
is 40
and doesn't talk to anyone
you
will die
and nobody will ever read your shit
and
I'm fine with that.

I write like this but it's not true

all this shit I write down like this
in this poem form which aren't really poems
just stupid rantings
should be about how the world is awful and
dreary and people are mad and stupid and
the worst thing ever created
but
when they aren't
and they show some cheerfulness and hope about
my life
just know
it's for her
and
him

so
when I'm gone and dead in the fire
and
my ashes on are on some shelf somewhere or
in the sea

and they go back and read this shit
they
will know
I wasn't so unhappy about everything. because I really
wasn't
I was fucking elated about our lives together and I wanted
nothing more in life to spend
all my free time with both of them…

I just think it's more fun

to tear the world into shreds
and
say that

WERE ALL GOING TO DIE VERY SOON
AND IT'S ALL OUR FAULT!!!!!!!!

and I don't think I'm alone.

we love it

it's like Christmas morning
like when I was 10
I wake up
check my phone
and
hope
hope
hope
the game hit the under
or
the QB passed over 240 yards
and
if it goes my way
I jump up and down
happy
as hell
yes yes yes yes yes
this is the happiest I've ever been!
what the fuck
is this life?
how did I get here?
football is life
no
betting is life
we
all love it
we all die by it
it makes life exciting
other than that
what else do we have?
just

don't
kill yourself over it
it's not
worth it.

what happened?

the part of my brain
that
is responsible for talking
might be breaking down
as I get older
or
more
isolated
and
yet
when I sit down to type
at the keyboard
late at night
kind of drunk
I can put it down
better than ever
it's like
I'm a genius
it's like I'm Billy Joel
playing piano
that mother fucker
who
can play by ear
that's
what its like
and then
when I need speak…it's so god damn hard!

he don't care a bit and I love it

"have you ever seen "Five Easy Pieces?"

I asked my father
who
was born in 1955
and
graduated high school in 1973.

"no…what's that?"

and I shook my head

again…because I already knew what he would say…

how is it possible I've seen more movies in his age
in his generation than him?

ONE OF THE BEST MOVIES I'VE EVER SEEN
AND HE HAS NO IDEA WHAT IT IS!

and then
I calm down
I stop
caring
because
movies don't matter do they? he lives life…I watch
movies
and
there is a difference…

it was there the whole fucking time

the
whole
fucking
time

just
pick up a skateboard
and
learn it!

you don't need anybody!

just you and that stupid board!

I could have been so much more…

and then
later (right now at 40 years old)
I saw the error in my ways…

those skaters
they were so cool

long shirts
smoking pot
getting girls
cool, dyed hair

they hated everything like I did
but
they could do ollie's and board flips and

all that other bullshit

and the girls! so many stoner girls loved those skaters!

I already dressed like a bum
and
had that skinny body with the bad hair
and
horrible teen mustache…

why the fuck didn't I buy a skateboard at 12 years old and
practice it in my driveway everyday for 3 years
and then
by the time I got into high school
I could have been so much cooler…right?

and then
and then
and then
I think about all the stupid drugs

doing them at 13, 14 or 15

like my cousin Jeff
who
got wrapped up

smoking weed early on
smoking cigs
drinking

all while getting together in a church parking lot
skating around

with a bunch of goons and
white trash whores

and all I did was idolize him

when I was 12 and he was 14

I was doing nothing…I was too nice…and

then
10 years later

he ended up on the needle
horribly addicted

had some kids
then did some time
for theft

lost his relationship with his daughters

everything crumbled

all while I stayed the course, stayed alone, just
bided my
and
finally got to college and started drinking
like a normal kid
then
everything was ok…

and
I'm now happy I never skated…at that beginning of this poem

I had a different opinion which is crazy.

FUCK THAT SHIT!

but what if my boy wants to skate…God what will I say?

I want him to be cool but I don't want him to be a fucking drug addict!

so what do I SAY?

top 10 books that make me happy

Ham on Rye
(the goat writes his life story and we all bow down)
Great Gatsby
(I keep reading this and keep wanting to put myself in the
place of Nick Carraway, thinking it would be so interesting
being in the middle of all these insane rich people who have
no idea what to do with their lives and they are all miserable.)
Flowers for Algernon
(the only book I've ever cried to)
Slaughterhouse Five
(Vonnegut, he got it right. this guy, he's here but he's not. we
all
run, we all want to be away from where we are, so this is this
guy's life
he travels time, goes back and goes forward and into outer
space
like about doing! it's fantastic!)
Rosemary's Baby
(never been into horror novels but this one, it isn't a horror
novel, it
fucks with your head it's so simple and easy to read and keeps
you
wanting more)
Ishmael
(an assignment my sophomore year, it opened up my mind
told me the truth and it's my new bible)
Ready Player One
(anyone who played video games in the 80's and 90's would
love
this book because this guy knows his shit and we all want to
go back

to that simple time, this fucker, he nailed it)
Confederacy of Dunces
(tried to read it three times before I finally got past the first
few chapters
and then…it opened up, like a mother fucker, it finally made
sense
that fat bastard who hated himself…he figured it out)
1984
(Orwell…the man…the prophet…he knew what would
happen…but couldn't predict
his own death…the fucker.)

I'm so glad

when Eli gets old
in his
early 30s

and I'm still a fucking drunk
he's going to say to his girlfriend

he's a good drunk. he's such a nice guy who fix
anything and he never missed a day of work
and
he loves his wife and he loves me and he
still runs at 65…

but yes
he
drinks

ALL THE TIME.

HAPPY NEW YEAR!!!

finally
one
thing
we
all
agree
upon
and
nobody
is
fighting
about
what to
say…now more of that shit…

another one

this film or movie or indie or whatever
you want to call it…another hour and a half
THING

where it's all good looking quirky white people
who are kind of working but not really and
they are writing and involved in art and plays
and living in this amazing picturesque New York City
which doesn't really exist and the apartments are big
and should be very expensive but they aren't because
it's a movie

I LOVE THESE FUCKING MOVIES. THEY ARE THE
FARTHEST
THING FROM REAL LIFE, FARTHER THAN SUPER HERO
MOVIES
BUT I DO LOVE THEM SO

it takes me back
back
back
to that simple time
when
I met my first wife
when she was in art school
when
things were so stupid and good and
easy
and
40 seemed like a million years away

so gimme them
gimme them
I'll watch them on my nice big couch
in my nice big house
in my lap of luxury

so
I can feel like I'm back in that
old world

for just a little bit…like an hour…and that's ok…

without the smell!

people are people are people

I'm pretty much an idiot
even though
I talk all this shit
about knowing what people
are like and how they function
and why
they do the things they do

which is all
horseshit

don't listen to any of it.

the only thing I know
is
if you think you are better than
everyone

NO ONE LIKES YOU AND YOU
PROBABLY DON'T GIVE A SHIT
ANYWAY

and that's about half the world
right now

                                        the rest of us
just trying to make it day to day
without pissing off the wrong
people

and
it's always has been that way.

keep going

how long can I go on like this
it's a good life
I have it all
but
many before have died early
and
yet
I go on
like nothing
no
consequences
so
maybe just keep doing what I'm doing until
I see a crack
because
if I stop
it may
cause some kind of avalanche of shit
the body
is used to this lifestyle by now
so
keep going
just do it
it makes you happy
so
just keep going.

used to be fun

you go into that place you used to go at least once a week…it's
been a damn
long time since you've been back…a good few years…and
now you are a different
man…a man whose grown and has a new wife and a child
and is living the GOOD
life…you look around at those poor people…all down and
out…in a different light
now…you aren't one of them anymore and it makes you
sad…you used to love
entering the store and exclaiming "MY PEOPLE!" in your
brain and then going to
look for cool t-shirts and vintage video games and weird
artwork…and now stroll around on
your lunch break like you are a stranger in a strange
land…wondering if you were
happier back then or now…you peruse the shirts…you still
like them…you will
always like wearing goofy shit…and you find a few for 3
bucks a piece and head to the
front to pay and there's a giant line…people with carts full of
clothes and only two
registers open…you only have 10 minutes to get back to work
and it's going to take
at least a half hour to get out…and you are sad when you put
the shirts back on some
random shelf and walk back to your car because you really
wanted those shirts but
it's not worth it…the poor fuckers…all standing
around…smelling like shit standing

around with their arms full of useless junk…they will
probably never make it out…they
are too nuts…I was just young and now I'm fucking old and it
isn't fun anymore…

that day

that summer day…I think 2002
fucking hell
we sat there
listening to Sublime
on the porch
smoking cigs
taking down
Yeungling beers
with an occasional whiskey shot
and then
"Summertime" comes on the air
and it's the most perfect moment
we talk about
how good we have it at the moment
we are
IN THE FUCKING PRESENT TIME for a few minutes
we are happy
which never ever happened in my life
ever
even though we had our whole lives ahead of ourselves…

I still feel that day
now
I can transport myself because it was such a great day
in my life
and it's funny
because it was so ordinary
at the time.

go ahead and try and take it away

it's all bad out there
this country going to hell
but
here we are
on Sunday
again
it's fall
weather is beautiful
football is still great
and
I don't know if they will ever be able to fuck it up
as much
as they've tried over the year

it's always going to be football…

let the world burn down…I don't give a fuck

keep playing
and
well be happy

take over the country

just keep playing
and
we won't care

football is the essence and nobody can take it away from us…

entertainers we are not

we sit there
machines humming along
the three of us, staring at the wall
trying not to look at each other
nothing to say at all, all dreading our stupid lives
attached to this job, this building, this stupid workplace
where we spent most of our lives at this point
I think…fuck…why don't we start chatting, like in all those
podcasts I listen to…it could be so interesting talking about
shit going on in the world, movies, television, conspiracy
theories,
our backgrounds, childhoods stories, books, video games,
hobbies…all of it!
but no, we are all uninteresting idiots who have nothing to say
to anyone. we just sit
and wait…thinking about what we are going to eat for lunch
and what we are going
to eat for dinner and watch when we get home…

easily top 5

watching these old movies
from the early 1900's
they were all smoking
in all buildings and houses without any
air conditioning
looking hot and bothered
puffing away
to fill the time
and
what a time it was! we think…oh it looks
so much fun
being able to light smoke after smoke
without any
thought of consequence!

it's not a bad trade off, if you think about it.

air conditioning might be the greatest invention
in the history of man

easily top 5

so who would trade all that cool comfort
to be able to buy 10 cent packs
and spark up
at any place at any time (planes, classrooms, work offices,
god damn hospitals!)?

many of us, I believe.

wisdom comes at a price

these retired porn girls
we think they are 45
but
really they are 29
because they have
been through it all
since
the age of 12
and
they have more wisdom
than
a 70 year old who had
an easy
normal
life.

A.R.P.

he seems so cool, even though
he's a total nerd. but he made it. he
went to NYU film school and made little
movies and then his own black and white
goofball comedy ala Kevin Smith on his own
dime and now he's a successful respected
independent filmmaker and he's still that same
Star Wars geek he was in high school but now that
he writes and directs indie movies, he's so cool, he's
so fucking cool to everyone. and you want to be him
but you know you will never do any of that shit so
you try and pretend by dressing like him and talking
like him and writing like him and reading Phillip Roth
and telling people you like obscure old horror movies from
the 70's and 80's
even though it was never your thing and it will never
be your thing and after a while you feel like a fraud
emulating this guy and one day you realize you need to
stop, just take one thing about him you like, one thing
that you think will make you look cool and do that, so
you decide that the one picture he is wearing these awesome
sunglasses and you will find a pair that looks like that and
nobody
will ever know where you got the idea and it will seem like
you
are creative and unique and then
live your life without trying to be anybody else.

can't compete
you walk into the bathroom
and you really don't have to pee but
you are going to be inside working with the big machines
for a while
so you gotta get that little last bit out so
you open the door and some man you work with
is pissing at the urinal
like a real man
big, loud stream coming out
so
instead of standing next to the guy
and trying your best to get that little trickle out
you dart right for the stall…

and then later, hours later
you got a bag full of piss
and some guy is at the urinal
trying to get anything out
you choose a different path…

coming back again

you're at the point
where you are so drunk
nothing matters
like back in college
it feels so good
so
fucking good
you put on an old song from the 90's
like
you are back in the dorms
fuck everything
I don't care if I am poor
I need a cig
what the fuck!
is how we feel
and it's the most honest we've felt
in
10 years
if only the wife could understand…

sleeping baby

finally
finally
finally

here I am
6am

he's still sleeping
soundly

in our bed though
with the woman

he hates that crib
that prison

he loves his mama too much.

we know
he should be in his own room in his
box of bars

but
what the hell ya gonna do?

HE'S FINALLY SLEEPING!

FINALLY!
FINALLY!
FINALLY!

and now I can relax
here
at my desk
in my
own room

like I'm 10 years old again

with all this goofy shit on the walls
surrounded by books

with my computer
loaded up with
all my old video games from the 80's and 90's.

and
a sketch pad by my elbow
as I type.

life is pretty good right now.

all those years

fuck you! I won't ever use that stupid thing!

I said.

it's just rain
it's just water
who cares if I get a little wet…it's better than
looking like
a wimp
holding this invention made for women!

I'm too tough
for that!

I said.

and then

20 years go by…

the man gets married. he has a child. he's secure. he has a
great
job.

he doesn't need to be cool. he doesn't need to be tough.

he goes out to his car
before work and it's raining like crazy.

fuck.

he stops at the drug store on the way to work and pays 10
bucks
for an umbrella.

he feels like he lost.

FUCK.

and then

he exits his car and

opens this female product
and
walks through God's climate

he's feels better than he has in
all his life

he's beat nature…why the hell didn't I do this
before?

why?
why?
why?

it's so convenient!

but that image…of a man…with that cover over his head…

it was supposed to be an hour long job.

I've done it before. on the drivers side, now the passengers
side
wheel hub was squealing like pig.

easy.

take the wheel off
take the brake caliper and bracket off.
take rotor off
take the axel bolt off
and then
behind the hub
there are three bolts. 15mm. just get a socket behind there
and get them out.

should take a half hour to get them off
a half hour to get the new one back in.

easy.

and then
2 hours later
the three bolts behind the wheel hub
are stuck.

I sprayed four different lubricants
to try and loosen them up
but
they are in there like cement.

fuck!

what the hell do I do? I need to get this done
today because I have to work tomorrow.

I hate working on my daily driver. it's not fun.

so
I think about calling my dad. he can always get these
bolts out. he's been doing it his whole life and even though
he's
on his way to 70, he's got this knack
as do a lot of guys his age do, who grew up in that era of
muscle cars.

I pulled out my phone and got ready to text…no. no I said.

just wait. it's too easy. you can do this yourself. he's not
going to be around forever and I have to figure this out.

so
I took a breather. had some lunch. took a shit. came back out
and
took it one bolt at a time. little by little, it came out. quarter
turn
by quarter turn, it was coming.

and then
15 minutes later it was out.

VICTORY! a small one, but that's what it was.

I could do this. I knew it now. I still wanted to call him to help
me out because I love my dad and I like working on cars with
him but I had to do this on my own…

2 more.

they seemed to come easier. slow but easy. I had the
confidence
and that's all you need when going up against a 2001 Buick
Century with
bolts rusted and seized like no other.

an hour later
it was a beautiful thing. driving down the street…all quiet…

I did it. I saved 400 bucks. fixed my car in my driveway on a
nice day
wrenched the shit out of it

like some backyard redneck mechanic…like I am.

just some people dying, whatever

we see real murder
almost everyday on the internet
and
it doesn't bother us
whatsoever
anymore
because we don't know these people
even though
they are innocent humans
just trying to go about their day
and
it could be any of us
but
WE DON'T CARE!

but if it was one of our family or friends…

my wife

she found her dad
who overdosed on heroin
upstairs
when she was 16 years old
on the day she took off of school to go out and have
fun with him on "daddy daughter day"
and
she's the most normal, most stable woman I've ever
met

and she said she never got any therapy for it
nobody at school ever asked her about it
her mom never talked about it
teachers
students
nobody said anything.

she held it in and grew up and
made a life for herself
like a normal person
which
makes no sense
when I think about my easy life
and nothing like that ever happened and I'm
insanely depressed sometimes…

she's one of the strongest people I've ever met and
that's why I love her more than anybody on the planet…

at the edge of the bed

almost falling off
the baby
my son
my beautiful boy
my annoying but amazing child
is
          trying to push me off
and
it's the middle of the night and I can't help but think
of a few years back when I had this whole king bed to
myself

I would lay right in the middle and sprawl out totally naked
and jack off and sleep in
every fucking day and it was the most amazing thing
ever
feeling like an old king
from back in the day
it's was almost heaven
for a week…

and then
it became ordinary. it became lonely. it became nothing
and
I'm back in the now
where I have on leg off the bed and I want to
push the baby back to the middle but he might sleep
and
I'm so happy that I'm here now, I'm good, I have love
and
only God can take that away and if he does then I deserve it

so
let's just sleep here
uncomfortably
thinking, one day, this little boy will be sleeping his own bed
and I'll
be back in the big bed with the wife and
ILL HAVE IT ALL!!!

the rest of us

you see all these people walking around
the store
driving their cars
to and from god knows where
all of them
most of them
no
all of them
they are either really good at their jobs
and
they pay for everything to be done
in their personal lives
and they avoid their families as much as
possible and drink and do drugs and
wish for eath
and
can't deal with anything real in life
outside the work

or
they are good at nothing
god damn
nothing

and they
just float on by
in life
feeling relaxed and happy they
have it very easy

and they will live almost forever

while the rest of us
those in the middle
who
are ok at work
and
ok at home
who
are a jack of all trades
we
die of anxiety at the age of 45
because
cancer got us
from that damn stress...

I'll say it again
over
and over and over and over
and
over

it feels so good

to be lazy
so lazy
not doing anything
you know you need to wrap it all this shit
pay bills and clean and get gas and
get food and do all this other crap
but
you let it go
and then
one day
you decide
I'm tired of living like this! so
let's get it all done in 2 days
and it's a hurricane of bullshit
and then
when it's all done
on a Sunday night
you think
thank the fucking Gods
I finally got off my lazy fucking ass to fucking do it
      allllllllllllllllllllllllllllllllll!

soon enough

you look around
at all this shit
that used to give you joy
10 years ago
no
30 years ago
when you were a kid
and
you just got it back
as an adult
to relive your childhood
and now
it's just shit. it's stupid stuff…it's meaningless
and
you feel horrible
not even human
you hate yourself
because you can't even
enjoy life anymore
and then
you see your baby…he will like it! one day!
so well keep it around for a while!
and then
WELL ENJOY IT TOGETHER!!!!!

just for me

I think all these poems are worthless
and then
I look at my bookshelf and see
almost 40 books
full of my words
with those
nice covers
I designed myself
and I'm drunk and I pull off
one of them
and I read a short one
and
I laugh
thinking
wow that wasn't bad!

and I'll keep going with this even
though
nobody will ever see this…

bad bad yes bad

the ass has bleeding for 2 weeks
bad
bad
bad

like looking down at an abortion everytime
I release

and
she knows all about it

apparently it's a fissure, an tear in my ass
and

she's still here
so
what that means is she will be here till the end

nothing can phase her

and
I would understand
if it was the other way around.

stay home or fly commercial

these stupid rich fucks
who are
addicted to
private
air travel

they will all die
eventually

another jerk off
some
rap producer asshole
who
chartered his own jet

ALL DEAD.

the kids the wife
himself
his staff

ALL DEAD.

stop it. you will die. just go commercial. I know it's hard
just
stop
thinking you are better than us because you have money
it's not worth it
YOU WILL DIE.

and I'm alive

here
typing
drinking a ton
because I STAYED HOME. SO FUCK YOU.

comes around

life is cyclical
        for all us
we don't change
we think we do
but
we are still that same person
deep down
it's still us
no matter
how much we dress ourselves up
no matter how much money we make
no matter how good we look
no matter how many people we fuck
no matter what car we drive
no matter where we live
we are that same person
and
it's always going to come back to us
that shit
we enjoyed
that nerdy stupid shit
those girls we used to like
that bad food we used to eat
we can never get out of it
it's in us
        until we die…

those bastards

who choose art over real life
they give it all to the craft
they don't give a fuck about anybody
it's all about being a creative genius

we worship them
and
never care what they do to the people
in their lives
torturing them
making everyone around them miserable
so
they could "create" amazing works of art and film and books
and
music

the big 4

but
do the people in their lives

do they appreciate the shit they created? or do they hate
it all?

they do love the money though
when they are gone

they love that money and legacy….they love it….it's at least
something….

it always happens

so drunk
and
I want to reach out to everybody

but
when I'm sober
most of the time

I don't talk to anybody
except my wife

I stay silent…

what would I do if I ever stopped drinking?

would I feel the need to reach out?

ever?

or
would I stay in my shell
like
the shy turtle I am?

god
I hope I never stop boozing
it's

so
fucking good

it's everything…sometimes…

we had no chance in hell

you had a dream where you saw her again
in some other dimension
like that other time line in *Back to the Future*
things were very different
we were both single and there were no problems
and
everything was perfect
and
then the alarm went off
and
you barely remember what the hell happened
you will never know
only
she was there and it was strange because
it all worked out in the end

Bill and Dan and Harold

watching *Ghostbusters 2*
on basic cable
should be a horrible experience
based on what we all thought of it
when it came out
back in the day
but
now
with all these shit movies
the last 10 years
it's actually a great fucking movie
compared to all this shit
they shove down our throat
nowadays
and I know I sound like an old man and nothing could make
me happier!

back nine

I always told her
"listen, after 40, anything can happen, we can
die at anytime, especially men."

and she didn't believe it.

"no!
that's crazy!"

and then
last week
her friend from college
who was married with 3 children
she said her husband was diagnosed with
brain cancer
at 43 years old…

see, I told you!

I wanted to say. but I didn't. I couldn't. I wouldn't.

it was too depressing. thinking about those young kids, aged 5
to 10
losing their father in possibly a year to five years…

what the fuck!

this shit…this life….why even try? if we do all we can do be a
good
person
live a clean life

like her husband
and then
get hit with a Mack fucking truck
out of nowhere

what the fuck is the point? why build it up like that?

might as well
do heroin
and
die at 30

fucking shit. fucking shit hell. it makes no sense...

were all doomed. it's pointless. but
we keep going on
thinking we will live forever
and
that's how it is
because
otherwise
nothing would get done
nothing would get built...we have to trick ourselves
that
were keeping it all going for our grandchildren
who
won't give a fuck
either.

freedom is important

so
I would tell anybody
take your time
don't have kids too soon
because
once you do
it's over
you can't do anything anymore
except be a parent
unless you are one of those scumbag people
who
leaves their family
so
just wait till 33. it's the perfect age. gives you time to
have 2 kids and you have a good
10 years after college to pay off your debt, buy a house
and build a career.

it's nothing to them

these guys
who can be friends with the hot
girls at work

I don't know how they do it…

it's so natural to them
they get along great

I can never do it…all I think is
if that was me

I couldn't stop thinking about
fucking them
and
I would ruin my marriage
because
anytime a good looking girl gave me any attention
in life
I wanted to marry her!

so
I stay away.

and
then
I imagine
the guy
will eventually cheat on his wife
with the young girl
and

then his wife will die
because
I watch too many crime shows…

the young artist girl

she's so hot
she's so cool

you are intrigued…who is this person
and why
do I need to be near her
all the time?

she's such a good fuck
you think
I could do this forever!

and then

after 2 weeks…

you are out the door

you've seen past her curtain.

if it was easier, then maybe

The band Tool
is touring again
after all these years
has to be
15 by now, maybe 20?

I don't know. they might have
been around at some point
from 2003-now
but I wouldn't have known…too much life
was happening…but now?

the money problems are over
the house problems are over
the work problems are over
the wife problems are over

it's all about the baby now
which
is a simple kind of life
dealing with this one child
but we don't get out as much as we did
which can get kind of addictive
being in this very comfortable prison
with and endless amount of television to
watch
on big comfy couches with good food and
drink.

so when I saw that the band Tool was touring again
I immediately texted my college buddy

Lomack
and he said
HOLY SHIT!! WE'VE GOT TO GO!

I almost text FUCK YEAH right away but then
I thought about it
the whole rigamarole of going to a giant concert like that
in jersey (because he lives in jersey)

the two hour drive there
the getting totally wasted
the taking off work
the sleeping at his house where his wife and two children live
the waking up with a hangover
the two hour drive back
and worst of all
the wife worrying the whole time I would do something
stupid
and then
I texted back

YEAH, GOTTA SEE THEM NOW BECAUSE WHO KNOWS
WHEN
YOU WILL HAVE A CHANCE

and that was it. I left it at that. I'm happier I didn't commit.

I can still go back in my mind
all the times we saw them back when we were in
college and all the songs were amazing

but now
the last two albums weren't that great

so
half the concert would be shit I wouldn't like

so thank god I stepped back and actually thought about
what it would be like to go to a concert like that
at 40 years old
and I don't care how pathetic it sounds
I will usually choose the easy
path
because it's easier.

not really

now that the internet has taken over the world
and we are locked away in our houses
to avoid this horrible pandemic virus
everyone is becoming a recluse
like I have been my entire life
so
I can say

at least I'm not
alone
in wanting to be
alone

but really
we want to be connected to people
just
not in real life.

she never complains

the trash bag has fallen down
only one corner is holding on
and instead of pulling it up
which takes one second
the garbage has piled up on top
and after a few walk bys
I finally say to myself
if I was at home, I would have pulled this up
by now but it's work so we expect some
magic cleaning fairy to come by and empty it
but the poor woman is currently down the hall
cleaning the horrible mess in the men's bathroom
so I take 15 seconds and push the trash to one
side and pull up the bag and secure it to all
four corners. I step back and feel like a god damn
hero without a cape. she won't ever know I helped
her out and that's ok. she probably won't even
care because even the can was overflowed with
old food with the bag far below, she would just
do what I did without a thought because she's so
used to us children making these messes we don't
want to clean up.

**all I want is all I need and I never seem to get there but now
I feel good**

and it comes out
and
everything is going to be ok
for the next few hours
you feel like a million bucks
take all the money in the world and
you can have it
if you could feel like this all the time
so
empty and easy and free
I wouldn't care about being rich at all!
keep every cent
I'll be poor
as long as I can GET IT ALL OUT LIKE A NORMAL
PERSON!

IT'S

"CUT THE GRASS"
AND
"MOW THE LAWN"

YOU CAN'T MIX AND MATCH THE TWO

YOU CAN'T SAY
I'LL

"CUT THE LAWN"
NO!

YOU CAN'T SAY
I'LL
"MOW THE GRASS"
NO!

IT'S EITHER OR
YOU CAN'T MIX AND MATCH...I prefer

cut the grass. it's very 1950's manual lawn mower.

mow
seems so harsh with giant machines. even though I use a
snapper rider
like Forest

I like to picture myself back in the mid 20th century.

cut...like scissors...
it seems so much

simpler. I like that.

musical or not? NOT

writing used to be so amazing
but now
it's just
ordinary
it's like taking a piss
I've written too many words
it's like
playing piano
I type and it comes out and I have
no idea what
it produces
which
is fine
fine
fine

who cares?

ordinary routines by ordinary people

he goes out and warms up his truck
every damn day
like the rest of us stupid fucks who are still
actually going into work
but
he's doesn't have a job. no. he's a war vet in
his 40's and has some type of disability now
and doesn't work. but he goes out and gets
that cup of coffee everyday
at 7:15am. sometimes he's a little earlier
and I catch him coming back from Wawa
and I give a wave…sometimes he's late and I catch him going
out to start it up and other times he's right on
and the car is already warming up as I drive by his house. and
then
as I'm driving home, by his house, he's usually out walking
the dog with a big coat and hat with a cigar in his mouth…I
give a wave and I'm on my way.

I'm obsessed with him as I am with many ordinary people
doing ordinary routines that boggle my mind.

but then
I put myself in his shoes. no job, at home all day, I might
be doing the same thing, getting out of the house as much
as I could, going to get coffee, Walmart, the grocery store, the
auto store, the thrift store. what the hell else is there to
do in the dead of winter? you can only watch so
much TV without feeling like a lousy bum.
so
it does make sense. but I still find it funny and I'll

keep focusing on this man.

in other roles under the same direction

I think I prefer the directors who use
the same actors in their movies
to the ones
who do the opposite
who
have to have a new crop of people
in each movie they do
even though the former
has to be waaaaaaay easier
but the exception might be Kubrick
who
I don't think use one of the same actors
in any of his movies…he could do
no wrong.

hard wired

so these people were making this documentary
on shaming people
and they wanted to see if people enjoyed
watching people fail or watching people succeed
so
they hooked up these wires to their face and showed
them
their soccer team scoring goals
and they all smiled and cheered
but then
they showed them clips of their rival team
missing goals
and
they cheered even more
and
it shows what we already knew
that
humans are hard wired to bask in the failure
of others
we love it
it's like cocaine
it's what we live for
but why?
my theory is because it's so easy. we don't have to do
anything. succeeding in life takes a shit load of work
but
hearing about your neighbor losing his job
is effortless
and
it makes your life seem so much better
while you sit and watch TV.

it would be so easy

pulling off one of my old poem books off the shelf
I can't believe how wacked out of my mind
I was
drinking
everyday
single
wishing I was getting laid
fucking beautiful women
but really just going to work and
jerking off way too much
I'm amazed how normal my life is now
with the wife and the kid and the nice house
it
doesn't seem real
we just had a nice Sunday of cooking a nice dinner and
watching football with the baby crawling around like a
bandit…

and then I think for a second

what if it all goes away? I could be back there
in a second
can't I?

and then I get scared for a moment…how the hell could I
function without my family?

I can't, I can't, I can't go back!

and then I realized that I could actually do it
that thing I wanted to do my whole life

that terrible thing
that would make my parents cry forever…

in for the long run

you see them running
at all hours of the day
driving to work
at 7am
they are on the side of the road
they jog by and you see that look on their face
it's always the same
pure despair
like they are in fucking hell
it's because they are
and then
driving home
in a rain storm
there they are
rounding a curve
with that look of misery
in some terrible plastic poncho
and neon short shorts
looking like they want to kill themselves
but
this running
this is getting them through
one more day
everything in life is the worst
we have no idea why we are here or what
our purpose is
except running. it's the only thing that makes sense…it makes
us
happier than anything in the world but to get to that
happiness
we have to endure this awful exercise

day in
day out
just get it done, and then
when you are in the shower
that feeling in your brain is like no other. it's better than
any drug or sex or food or whatever the fuck else you can
think of…you are done for the day
thank God…but tomorrow will come and with the sunrise
comes
that damn lifelong commitment.

I wish it wasn't

it's true
no matter how much money you have
no matter how big your house is
no matter how many cars you have
no matter how many beautiful women you have
no matter how great your adult life is

it doesn't matter

you will always be miserable. you will always look back
back
back
back
to your childhood
when
it wasn't all corrupt
when
you had no idea how money worked
when
if you had 15 cents to buy some candy at the trailer park store
and
another 25 cents to buy a pack of baseball cards

it was the best time in your life…

like Kane…he had the right idea, with that stupid sled…he
had everything
in the world

but that stupid sled from when he was 10 was all he wanted…

you see

this rich beautiful young couple with the cutest little girl
dressed up like a princess
walking around Disney World and they seem like they are
living
some kind of dream life, and then you look at your life and
it's nothing compared to *that* and you start to feel bad about
your existence, like, what the fuck did I do with my life? why
didn't I work harder and drink less and not buy as much
stupid
shit and why did I choose to watch a movie when I could have
been learning the stock market and why did I play
Mike Tyson's Punchout!! when I could have been looking for a
model Russian bride on the internet
but then you think about the truth, you know the truth
because
even though you don't know these people at all, you know
someone
who knows them and it turns out they fucking hate each
other, they
don't have sex, they barely talk to each other…but these
pictures
they post online, they look literally perfect together with the
daughter
who lives a lavish life because the father and husband works
non-stop
because that's the only thing that gives him happiness…

it's the way things are now and I knew it would be this way

whenever I think back to
all those stupid things that seemed so important

back then
life was so easy

I had no idea

but really
I kind of did

because I kept putting off having a child
for a very long time

and now
actually having a baby

it's the only thing that matters
in life

keeping him alive and well and
mostly happy

everything else is bullshit
all those stupid things…

the video games, the movies, the drinking
the vacations, the cars, the books…

everything I thought that mattered
doesn't…

it's the baby. he's taken over life
like I knew would happen

but had no idea what it would be like
even though I tried to prepare myself as much as possible

nothing can compare you for waking up
every night for 2 weeks at 2am

to a screaming baby that seems like
it's possessed by some demon

and we both hold him and rock him and
give him a pacifier and give him a bottle and tell him it's ok

but he screams and screams and screams
not relenting…

and an hour later
he finally stops

we both are tired as hell

he's almost one and a half
why isn't he sleeping through the night yet?

hopefully tomorrow
I tell myself at 5am when I wake up feeling dead as hell

hopefully…

keep going even though it doesn't make sense

we're rocketing towards the apocalypse
not in the biblical sense but the climate sense
the earth destroying sense
trash everywhere, air, water all polluted
animals going extinct, forests being burned and torn down
to make way for farming
and as I walk out to my car at lunch
I look to my left and see this GIANT building
maybe 3 football fields long
men all over
like ants crawling around
welding and hammering and screwing shit
in
and all I can think is
why?
we all know it's coming to end. why do we keep pushing
forward like we will be here forever? we keep building and
buying and planning for a great future of humanity...for
what reason? what evidence do you have things are getting
better?
and
yet
I still write this shit. I should give up. shouldn't I?
the problem is we don't know when it's going to end.

could be a year, could be 50.

this company I work for is thinking the same
thing
so they keep going like humanity will never die.

and I guess that's what I think as well. everyday when I read
the news
it seems like we can't make it another week

and then
we do

so
here I am, typing away at 5:37am
because for some reason
as a species

we seem to endure…

made it out

we love all that music
where they sing about the dregs, the poor, the
awful shit in the world
         it sounds so romantic!
         oh God, I miss those old days!
         we had so much fun!
and yet
we have to get out, we hated living that *kind of life*
so
we work our asses off in our 20's
80 hours a day
not sleeping
drinking non-stop in our free time
it's a miserable existence
and
then 20 years later
we crank that gritty rock in our fancy cars
on our way to our giant house
thinking about how great it was
being young and poor and how much fun
we had going to the bar with all those
wild fuckers we worked with
and now they are all gone
some made it out, most are still killing themselves
now
in their 40's
listening to that music
wishing they were anywhere else in life
and
and
and

we smile a bit
knowing
unless shit gets really fucked up
we won't ever have to go back to that
        kind of life.

a new way of life, a better way of life

the writing
it has taken a back seat
to the bullshit of life
but
it's still there...it will always be there
in the brain
sentences are formed all day
and as long as I write some shit down
in a notepad
I'll get it down
sometime
when
everyone is asleep
it's the only way

they all have to be asleep
otherwise
they want my attention!

is that a bad problem to have? people love me and they
want to be around me!

and
I want to be in my room with beer and a keyboard
like some psychopath!

no
no
no
no

I don't want that. I like writing when they are asleep and I like
being with them when they are awake

it's a good life and I'm happy I have them

the boy and the wife

it's all I really have. I did the isolation shit and it was going
to kill me. these two fuckers keep me going

they keep me from pulling in front of a tractor trailer.

the world is horrible but
in this house

it's heaven and I can't complain about anything.

nobody reads this shit anyway. so who gives a fuck.

they have people for that kind of stuff

they do
they don't have to deal with much
they got that money
they have teams of people to deal with all the bullshit

anything you can think of
any problem in the world
they make a call
no
they have a guy who makes a call and it's fixed
magically

most of the time they don't
even know about these problems
it's
like living in heaven

they travel around and eat
delicious food
and drink amazing alcohol
served by the poorest of poor
on pristine white beaches
cleaner than me or you have ever seen
in our lives

and when
they finally return
from flying all over the world
to their many giant extravagant
mansions

everything is perfect. everything is clean.
nothing is broken.
fresh flowers in the kitchen.
lawn cut.
pool nice and warm and clear…heaven.

and
it's all maintained by
people for that kind of stuff.

funny stupid thoughts

we think we want to be alone
because it would be so easy and fun
but
this damn person
we live with and have
love more than anything in the world
who
can be annoying as shit
has become our entire world
and she's in my DNA now
which means she's essential to my survival on
this planet
so
any thought of going back to the way things were
5 years ago
is
totally ridiculous and I know
that she's not perfect
I am farther from it
than she is.

they turn their backs on themselves

hearing advice
from people in their 20's
          it's the best
they are just figuring it out…

fresh out their teens
just graduated from college
where their whole lives
it was all about trying to "be cool"
trying to look the part
trying to be some kind of interesting person
people talked about
and now
they are a little older
they see the world differently
now
they are working in a real job
and their lives aren't all about
socializing…it becomes all about money
and making your life the best it can be
so
they
say
shit
like
this:

"be your own person!"

"do what you do, don't listen to anybody!"

"if it makes you happy, then do it!"

and it's all so very true
and I laugh
laugh
laugh

because
weren't you the people
who
all you did was
do shit
to get attention from
anybody and everything?

the beer it's

taking effect
it's late
and
only an hour to go
before bed
time to put on music
enough of the bullshit of the world
enough of the talk
enough of all rational thought
just
give me the music!
god damn
tomorrow
is Monday and it will be all over!
fuck fuck fuck fuck!
Garfield was right!
what the hell, only 45 min now!
maybe
just grin and bear it, stay up another hour
and
enjoy life?

nah, nah, nah

nothing matters…does it?

we had all these dreams when in our 20's
about

our lives
20 years from then

and now

here were are
still working

haven't done what we wanted to do

in terms of enjoyment

sure
we have a house and child and married and
some stupid bullshit
but
that dream in your head

it didn't come true…did it? so maybe in another 20?

nah. you know now you will just be working the same
as now
still in debt…nothing much will have changed…cause people
are hard wired
from the get go

it's a damn shame…but it's better than living in some
awful poor country
so
we are winning always…aren't we?

I might never see them again

I'm thinking of them
kind of a lot
people from
a long time ago
from another lifetime ago
when we were just coming up
figuring out life
and
now we are all in our own lives
secure
making good money
spouses
kids
houses
deep deep debt
all that shit
and
all I wonder is
do they ever think about me?

it's good, it's good

sitting back
with the beer
empty stomach
dreams of nothing
so relaxed
listening to the old 90's shit
just like back in college
senior year
when
things calmed down
it was so easy
the pregame
was just me and the new roommate
after
Lomack graduated
I feel the same now
20 years later
it's so quiet
in the house
the wife and kid are settled, sleeping well
and
I have the house to myself
down here
watching football
it's easy
it's easy
I should be doing something
but
I am lazy now, I don't care
and I like it.
I love getting older

sometimes
there's no more
insane energy to conquer the world
we realized
there's nothing to conquer
it's all bullshit
were going to die soon
so
just relax
just chill
drink the beer
watch the game
(which is close)
and
be happy
things are the way the are
it could be so much worse.

and then
I sit back
and
take another sip
and
scroll through my phone (something
I didn't do back in 2003, because there were
no smart phones back then)
and
it's good.

I feel bad but I'm only human

almost asleep
trying to read this
supposedly great play

I even have a cup of coffee
to help me along
but it's not doing anything…

so I pick up my phone
for a breather
and
30 seconds later
my brain is on fire
I'm excited about everything on here!

what a jolt!

humanity is more insane than ever
and
it's all on display
on this stupid device!

how the hell can I go back to
the written word?

we are all screwed. it's never going back
to the way it was

not unless
we blow everything up
and

start from the beginning
again.

wasting the afternoon

watching old Corey Feldman commercials
from the late 70's, early 80's, before he
got Gremlins
it's fucking depressing
seeing him
so full of life
not knowing what the hell
his parents were doing to him
just going along with whatever
the adults told him to do…

and
then
videos pop up
showing him now
looking like a pale ghost of his
old self
looking plastic and when he talks
it's all about the past and how
he was abused and the drugs and
alcohol and how he had to divorce his parents
because they stole all his money…

it's god damn depressing…and then
you think it will be hard to
enjoy *The Lost Boys* or *The Goonies*
or *The Burbs* or
Stand By Me

knowing what we know now…but then
you put it on

and he's so entertaining!

so
then you forget and you say

well, at least he has some shit to look back upon
some
success

most of us
have nothing. so maybe he doesn't have it that
bad.

its now and its good

football is back
and
it's all we need
all day
the best day of the week
and
betting is totally legal
what the fuck else do we need?
nothing!
nothing!
nothing!
life is the best
so
you won't hear me bitching anymore
as long as I got my feet up
and
a cold drink
it's all good
it's all good
it's all good
fuck everything else
out there
the world can burn
and I'll be happy
watching these idiots
beat the shit out each other…

I feel normal

when I see Britney Spears now
at age 39
posting almost naked pictures
looking kind worn down and crazy as
hell and still in good shape
and then
I look at her pictures of when she was a teenager
looking insanely hot and a little crazy
and pretty much flawless
the funny thing is
I'm more attracted to her now
which makes me feel like
I'm never going to be that perverted old man
lusting after young girls
and that gives me some peace.

so much fun

sure, when we die,
it's the people closest to us
that well miss the most
but
then
you think about all that other shit

the food
the music
the booze
the tv
the drugs
the video games
the porno
the rollercoasters
the beach
the books

and so much more that makes us want to stay
alive forever

well miss all that stuff just as much

right?

putting a bow on it

the whole movie can be full of
amazing music
that coincides perfectly
with each scene
but
that song that kicks on
when the screen goes to black
and
it says

written and directed by

is the most important piece
in the whole film.

it's what we remember the most

and what well be humming
all week long at work.

it's a man's choice what to do with his money

gambling
like
anything else in life
is good

                                   in moderation
but
the perception is it's evil
and will lead you becoming addicted
like drugs
and then you will lose everything
like with drugs
but
I don't think that's the case. with all things it life
it can be controlled
and
thus
can be something that can be enjoyed immensely
turning
a normal hum drum boring fucking day
into one of the most exciting times
of your life…good or bad.

if a man works and has 100 dollars left over
after paying all his bills
and food and all that other shit

what's wrong with throwing it away
playing the horses or betting a football game
or
putting it on black with a spin of the roulette wheel?

sure
at the end of the year
that's 5200 you could have saved up
if you lost that 100 dollars every week
but
what the hell is the point
if you
are bored as shit
the whole time?

J. Andrew Thomas lives in the suburbs north east of Philadelphia, where he was born. He has a wife, a son and two toy poodles. He has written plays, novels, poetry and short stories which have all been self published. *Punching into Nowhere* is his 26th collection of poetry.

www.ingramcontent.com/pod-product-compliance
Lightning Source LLC
Chambersburg PA
CBHW061531120726
48001CB00004B/1491